By the same author

(as Tessa Stiven)

Poetry of Persons (1976)
While it is Yet Day (1977)

(as Tessa Ransford)

Light of The Mind (1980)
Fools and Angels (1984)

SHADOWS FROM THE GREATER HILL

TESSA RANSFORD

Photographs by Edwin Johnston

THE RAMSAY HEAD PRESS EDINBURGH

© Tessa Ransford 1987

First published in 1987 by
The Ramsay Head Press
15 Gloucester Place
Edinburgh EH3 6EE

Printed in Scotland by
W. M. Bett Ltd., Tillicoultry

ISBN 0 902859 94 3

*Published with the financial support of
The Scottish Arts Council*

HOLYROOD PARK AT NIGHT

Snow and solo, Holyrood park at night;
Flakes so brittle footsteps can press no print;
   Sky reflects the earthly pallor,
      Shadows of evening are blanched of darkness.

Star nor moon, no break in the haze of white,
Outline none to sharpen the lion crag;
   Wide terrain of hill and parkland
      Empty of creature beside my walking.

Round the frozen loch sleep the ruffled swans,
Geese and lesser fowl in their sheltering;
   Dogs and humans huddle safely,
      Lights of the city for hibernation.

Days are dark in winter, and nights are pale,
Blankly folded into each other's sphere;
   Even gulls are muffled, humbled;
      Silently I, alone, travel forward.

Far ahead I see, by the gate, the trees,
Hardened branches blurred by the pallid light;
   Nearly home I find beneath them
      Circles of softness where earth is warmer.

Friends grow distant, lost in their own distress;
Each of us alone bears what winter brings;
   Stiffened, frosted, leafless, upright,
      Yet, unawares, we make fonder patches.

FOR JEAN,
who grew alongside

MARCH 9th

Today
change was consummated.

Not knowing why or how
I had prayed I would be changed.

Sorrow took root
and grew a spindly tree
strapped for support
to my former self
and staked
in that nursery of pain.

Today
it was transplanted
into deep soil.
Its narrow shadow lies
in the oval grove.

MARCH 12th

I take his hand and hold
his head against my breast —

a bird, alighted
in the park,
a gull,
from wheeling high
against the dark hill
brightly.

MARCH 15th

The Ides of March blew white
blew horizontal
cut at every level,
routed out a resting place
on abraded ledges of the ruined chapel,
reduced to what endures
on its promontory.

Young trees:
ash, sycamore, beech, wild cherry,
plucked from their nurseries
in Armadale or Perthshire,
lifted with that soil still
mingled in their roots and
dipped in rich earth
to form a slender grove across the park.

Those young trees
stand
black, slim, sharp
at brave attention
on this their first trial.

Each reveals the code it carries
for shaping stillness
patterning sky.

Stand slight sentinels.
Guard new positions.
Draw yourselves up
to attain your height.
Now's no time for leaning,
for generosity.
The warm spring sun that fed your first days
and blessed your new placement with balmy pretences
has withdrawn today.

You must explore the dignity you dwell in,
hold to purpose
keep direction.
It will pass
this injustice —
and you will have grown.

MARCH 29th

Knee-deep in snow,
dark, wet, cold scentlessness,
old, tall trees
are striped white to windward.

Those young trees
have no roughnesses
for catching flakes
to build a thin streak
of snow-shading.

In a blizzard
none can run away that is rooted.
The wind does not relent,
drives cold in sideways,
etches black and white.

MARCH 15th

The Ides of March blew white
blew horizontal
cut at every level,
routed out a resting place
on abraded ledges of the ruined chapel,
reduced to what endures
on its promontory.

Young trees:
ash, sycamore, beech, wild cherry,
plucked from their nurseries
in Armadale or Perthshire,
lifted with that soil still
mingled in their roots and
dipped in rich earth
to form a slender grove across the park.

Those young trees
stand
black, slim, sharp
at brave attention
on this their first trial.

Each reveals the code it carries
for shaping stillness
patterning sky.

Stand slight sentinels.
Guard new positions.
Draw yourselves up
to attain your height.
Now's no time for leaning,
for generosity.
The warm spring sun that fed your first days
and blessed your new placement with balmy pretences
has withdrawn today.

You must explore the dignity you dwell in,
hold to purpose
keep direction.
It will pass
this injustice —
and you will have grown.

MARCH 17th

Sheer, white, fine light
of early sun on slight snow
wakes me —
and the young trees
self-consciously aware
of an ordeal undergone and to their credit,
of soft, separate snow melting at their base
and running to their roots,
of redshanks dipping overhead in twos and threes,
of Saturday in the park
as yet untouched, unhappened.

But my ordeal lies ahead.

I call in vigil
on whichever god or goddess
can take hold of serpents
and win their beneficence.

MARCH 21st

I love my books.
They are more consistent than men,
though they meet each changing mood,
companion my solitude.

Alone at night I search my mind
for a word on the page remembered
that never betrays,
a passage I once relied on
like daily bread,
a thought precisely expressed:
as I discover the plot
in which my part is played.

MARCH 28th

Three swans flew westward
in the filmy, cloud-white morning,
a triangle
a threesome like an arrow.

One is the swan of ambition
another the swan of emotion.
The third swan keeps the balance,
flies with cloudy, filmy patience.

MARCH 29th

>Knee-deep in snow,
>dark, wet, cold scentlessness,
>old, tall trees
>are striped white to windward.
>
>Those young trees
>have no roughnesses
>for catching flakes
>to build a thin streak
>of snow-shading.
>
>In a blizzard
>none can run away that is rooted.
>The wind does not relent,
>drives cold in sideways,
>etches black and white.

APRIL 3rd

The mountain keeps silent
omni-presiding
and wise trees wait wordless,

Words heap unuttered
crumpled inside me.

APRIL 5th

I glimpsed that red moon setting on Good Friday morning
6 a.m. directly face to face.
It sank behind the ridge without delay
in the corner of my just-opened eye.

It was burnished by what must have been the sun
rising, but I was too asleep to rise and
look towards the east. I let the moon slip
and myself slumber, in that early glow.

EASTER DAY

Darkness before dawn
and rain
rhythmical
encompassing within its sound
ourselves, the window ledges,
street and buildings,
cars, trees, grass, gate, wall.

It washes clean the mind
and cradles agitation.

We enter the temple of listening
where arabesque of birdsong
decorates the dawn
above the drumming peace,
the steady lethargy,
even the dull blessedness
of rain.

APRIL 13th

Rain diagonal
screens the mountain flank
in April, in daylight,
in sharp, clear stripes
against brown grasses
of a winter coat unmoulted,
except in muddy patches
where, long and damp,
it greens and thickens.

APRIL 16th

Trees do not grow
for three or four years
after being transplanted.
They settle their roots.

These trees in the park
are large to have been uprooted.
The younger the tree
the quicker it settles and grows;
so I am told.

My experience is different.
Roots were dragging me under.
I could not grow for the heavy clinging.

Transplanted now
I am lifted, winging,
weightless almost.

My growing is to shed
all that holds me down.

I grow stems of thought
to flower as poems.

APRIL 25th

The chapel ruin is in shade
on its level,
sheltered from the east wind
and rising sun.

The remnant wall faces north.

Window-gaps, like eyes,
still survey the centuries
and look at us
from every quarter.
They stare in shadow
or fill with quickening light.

I return the gaze
saying
'Yes, I soon shall pass,
while you remain.'

Yet traces of my abiding
may appear, with apertures
that take in sky and mountain.

APRIL 26th

Below my kitchen window
great, grey bricks were laid.

A team of workmen,
pinched and roughed by cold of early morning,
handed up bricks
crept along scaffolding
carried them to the building point
and stacked them.

Bricklayers took them
one by one
lifted and positioned them
on the wall they made to grow
line by line and
neatly turning corners —
no trial and error —
each one put precisely in its place.

MAY 1st

Today, the first of May
the sun was seen to rise
over contradictory cloud
at 5.30 in colour,

and young girls attended
silent
who had climbed the hill chattering.

As the orb achieved wholeness
they broke into dancing, singing
and running downhill to breakfast.

MAY 5th

To combine hard, dark, enduring substance
with here-today-gone-tomorrow blossom
within repeated cycle of foliage:
that is the fascination
(now I see it)
that is the satisfaction
in a tree.

Now I know why we worship them.
We see in them
our own toughness
and our weak extremities,
our own endurance and ephemera.

Young cherries stand in scant flower
calm in quiet roundels.

They chide me
not to look away
not to look with disillusion.

They demand humility
a self-forgiving smile.

MAY 7th

The hill is hiding its head day after day
and even at night
a strange indigo aura covers the peak.

The sun has not been seen
no more has the moon
in all this milky seedtime.

Gulls can hardly fly for weight of cloud.

Trees succumb to gravity
and people with grey resentments
sway and droop.

After so many days, to witness
the head of the mountain clear
its thoughts in order,
is revelation, an outline of truth.

MAY 20th

Summer makes the world soft
adds texture to birdsong.

The mountain gently nuzzles the sky.

Grass and trees conjoin
horizontal with vertical.

Insubstantial as shadow
the propped frame
of the ruined chapel . . .

Summer waives outlines,
merges soft on softness.

MAY 28th

Swifts spring from air
from nowhere
born of new light.

They exist in air, on air;
they follow the windstream from country to country
crossing turbulent oceans.

Seekers of longer light, wider space,
they skim the loch where swans shine
as waters darken and overturn,
trees sway low.

Do swifts believe in night?
They don't believe; they imagine:
they imagine life is a dance

space and light the music
darkness only the prelude
to more ethereal melodies.

JUNE 20th

The actual moment when
early in the haze of day
a quality appears of incandescence,

the whole world whitens,
hill slides slowly out of mist
swells towards intrusion of light.

I am invaded by that moment:
no annunciation
but epiphany; treasures

brought from history, humanity,
like golden weapons salvaged
from beneath the seas.

JUNE 22nd

Because when I wake to
gulls, traffic, sunlight, car-doors,
footsteps, voices, clouds, trees,
chirpings, clatters, my own smell and skin,
awareness of my awareness
bridged to you and back,
who are my now,
my words, image,
my pure, an icon,
figure of my truth,
who dreamt with me in sleep
so that it is
into you I waken. . . .

Because of this and the morning
I desire to speak your name,
not utter speech
but touch you with my voice
and hear the stroke of yours,
to know you there, there,
not far, yet far,
not here,
yet inward and immediate.

JULY 1st

Shadows from the greater hill
in early eastern light, project
upon the lesser slope, to fill
with dark its curves and hollowings —
as suddenly, without remark,
white gulls open huge black wings.

JULY 8th

'The love that spills out
of the too full cup . . .
The leftover love' (Alice Walker)

Women are designed with a capacity
that exceeds demand.
The demand cannot be forecast
and we are not found wanting.

I am no different
in my wispy, slender, Scottish
Asian, aching, striding,
enduring, joyous, anxious, hopeful
woman-shape.
Love melts from me
when it has once been lit.

Dido was no different
as much a queen as we are
whatever her colour or ours,
whatever her violent adventures,
her city raised from the sea
whose name remains a symbol
of *anima mundi* crushed.

Today the sun is high and strong and lasting.
The mountain is debonair.
I sense a distancing from me;
while in winter's cloak
it drew me closer.

My leftover love
cannot rain on the mountain.

The sky is blue and empty.
People sport in the park.
Even the little trees
need no consolation.

JULY 10th

A great dane is strolling in the park.
He lopes
left feet together
then right.

His head is high.
He feels in proportion
to the mountain.

Young trees fluster
inches above him.

His flanks are moving
in a strathspey.

His paces are longer
then those of his companion
who trips in jeans
and white, heeled shoes.

He keeps his distance
unable, quite, to own her.

JULY 11th

Just where they fell
sprawled in the park
on sunlit grass
a bike, a boy, a girl
in black, white and steel.

It is evening.
They do not move for an hour.

Their shadows move.
The boy and girl converse
heads together, feet apart.
The bicycle is silent.

JULY 27th

The view I am receiving
is through speckle of raindrops
bright but blurred
yet colours do not run.

All is screened
through blobbed transparency,
yet colours do not merge.

Mind is designed
to ask the world questions:
How far the mountain?
How new the trees?
How do we define the edge
between cliff and sky?

Where the colour changes I could fall.

Intensity of light
with degree of reflection
gives my eye a colour.

This mist is menacing:
it lets no contrast through
no way of judging action.

And I myself am moving,
mist or no mist,
ordered in my orbit.

Sometimes
by a stroke of thought
I am creating colour,
conjuring a contrast.

The view I am receiving
through my dotted window
I'll pick and choose
to colour now my life.

JULY 28th

Saturday
or is it Sunday morning?

Loud, collective clatter on the stair
and footsteps
changing their acoustic
when they reach the street.

AUGUST 1st

After the rains
gulls are fishing the grass
for worms.

They ripple over the surface
breasting the sunlight
and follow curves of the mower
where it circled the island of trees.

Worms are rising out of flooded tunnels.

It's easy fishing:
no need to scream and dive.

The hill is green and juicy;
it's never known so much moisture,
unaccustomed to luxury.

I'll paddle over the grass again
and catch medieval mushrooms
on the ancient duelling-ground.

AUGUST 3rd

The hill is tossing high, frail wisps of
rosy cloud to glide in steady gale
along a turquoise sky, around, above the
perpendicular and slightly askew columns,
above the triangular gap
between crown and crag.

The moon, full at midnight,
is now high and faded
almost a lazy eyelid:
day's eye opening
or night's eye closing.

Birds chase and ride the wind
reeling, wheeling,
aware that in a moment
ordinary flight of day will have to be resumed.

The hawk alone is steady,
keeps position despite the gale
to pinpoint a victim

and far below
grasses tinge in flower:
harebell, yarrow, lady's yellow bedstraw
among the rangy thistles and fatted doves.

AUGUST 4th

The night sky is like a Gauguin girl:
dusky and gorgeous.

The ancient chapel stands
narrow, gaunt,
inclined on its headland
like a bard or prophet
who would be harkened to.

I met the moon at eye-level
easterly and grainy
raising its amplitude
above the lower slopes.

AUGUST 11th

After dark, light
after dawn, grey
after wind, calm
after rain, dry.

A tiny white terrier scampers among the gulls.

A black speck of kestrel hovers among the clouds.

Beside the loch, trees are weary with their leaves.

Young trees, established, begin to lean slightly.

A jogger runs in red, with bare white legs.

As if from a tree-top I accept the scene
given each morning
calm, grey light.

I want no sudden sun,
no burst of rain or wind.
This peace, this unemphatic,
non-expectant, poised
detachment
I have worked for.

AUGUST 20th

The Duke's Fell ponies are out for exercise,
six in tandem pairs, with free-flowing tails:
Martin, Roy, Edward, Robin, Mark, Ebony.

They slow down beside me passing with my briefcase
in the prancing morning.

Each of them is power for ten times the buggy.
Six of them feel it not more than conscience
harnessed behind them,
but they know bit and blinkers, collar and straps.

Each of them is part of an all-black team,
moving with precision as one organism.

Their trainer speaks.
They hear his voice separately, but respond together.
The reins are in his fingers.

SEPTEMBER 7th

Leaves are black with density.

This breezy, Scottish muir
is turning into jungle:
sultry, wanting humour.

The hill remains monochrome, faded.

Even sound is muffled:
bird, dog, child, dream or conversation.

Motor engines, distant drills
raise their dull dirge.

SEPTEMBER 23rd

The loch has overflowed its banks.
The moon is overripe with juice.

Ducks were fed from this submerged pavement
and that lagoon was formerly the grass.

Water is taking to the road
and downhill to the traffic-lights.
What use are wheels?

Yet summer boats have gone
and swans return
with six enormous cygnets
to this enlarged domain.

One inch of rain
has altered our boundaries.

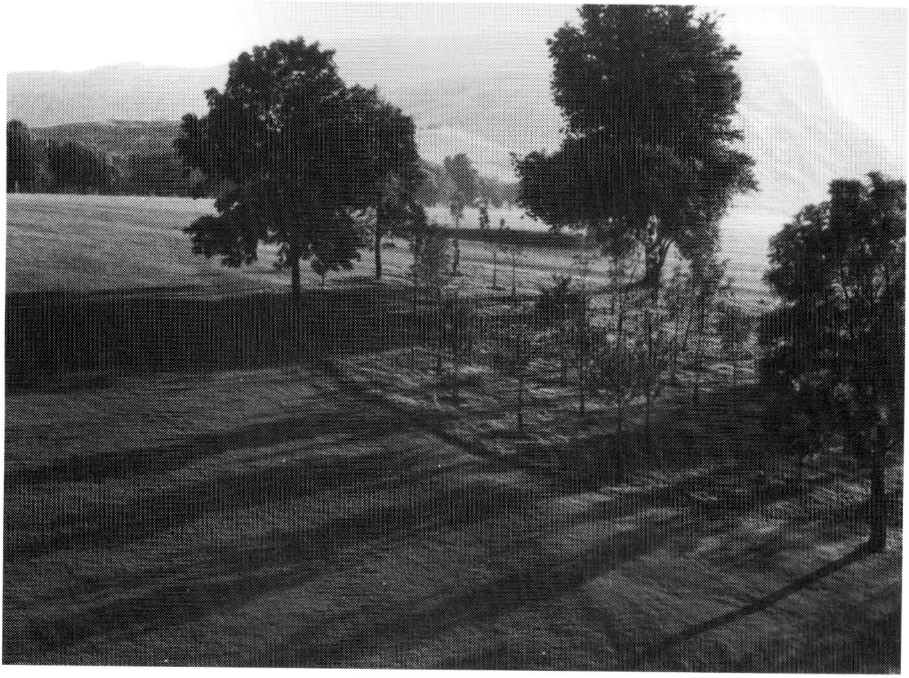

OCTOBER 6th

Tree in full leaf
wind in full blow
sun in full shine
make a shadow
that dances
dances.

Summer has gone
grass has grown
sky is clean
and darkly
the shadow-tree
dances.

Is this how Orpheus made trees move,
sun and wind his aid?

I applaud, and record
exactly this will never happen again:

I must hold them together
light and shade
wind and sun
grass and tree
impossibly dancing shadow.

OCTOBER 14th   (from Canada)

To define a particular mountain from this distance
across the Atlantic
is not difficult, since
no close-up obstacles can intervene.

Details must be omitted:
whether it rests in accustomed cloud
unperturbed, or rises
in clear, elegant outline of sun and shade.
The time of day, too, is slightly uncertain.

I know the time of year and how trees
are experiencing those first loving
touches of newly-awakened frost
which quietens autumnal trembling.
Beside the loch they are yellow
except for the willow,
but young trees in their roundels
are wispy and frail.
It takes a mass of withered leaves
for abundant colour.

The mower perhaps is working one last time
to leave the grass evenly smoothed
before the churning of winter.
Swifts have gone, but geese
flock and fly and land and walk and swim.
They own the place in their noisy way.
Birds are scarcely singing now
but berries are brilliant;
even beside the bus-stop on the roadside
haws are darkly bloody.
Rowans are dotted with crimson
as if welcoming winter:
its clear, piercing, crying, enduring love.

NOVEMBER 8th

In single file beside the loch
they fade, the trees, they tinge,
they do not shed their leaves
but manifest their branches.

How calm and green the scene:
it is as if
all manner of thing shall be green
and all shall be green
and certainly small is behovely.

I am framed by my window frame
again in Scotland,
waking to white flutter of gulls,
scruffy, friendly hump
of the multi-verdant mountain.

St Francis would have felt at home,
respectfully addressed it as 'big brother'?

NOVEMBER 17th

The sun at its zenith
is level with my windows.

It makes pale with pleasure
the park
and the last topmost
yellow leaves.

Young trees have shadows
like spokes
pointed due north towards me.

With massive stillness
the mountain hovers in shade.

Never in summer was this suspension:
a bird moves,
and silhouetted verticals
of tiny people climbing the mountain.

A cloud moves
when steadily watched.

NOVEMBER 27th

'The moon doth shine as bright as day'
and that is no
childish exaggeration.

The night sky is blue in piercing moonlight
and overhead
at great height
the Hunter's moon has reached
a zenith
of light and cold and clear and star and
I sleep strangely
waking to morning's darkness.

NOVEMBER 30th

No bird can peck so thick a frost.

Grass is hard, clod brittle.

A thin dawn has thrown gulls
    from cliff edge,
    tinged the sharp
mountain whose rock attacks the sky.

Blackbird, thrush, push tamely
among dead leaves, scavengers.

The parkland silent, silver;

among trees a piece whiter
    of soil
where frost nestled closer.

Last leaves shall fall surely?
Yet they hang, cling with berries.

I look clear, far
inhale with greed cold air.

DECEMBER 4th

I closed my eyes
and lay down in sickness.
When I opened them
trees were grey and naked —
even the tall willow
that was green the day before.

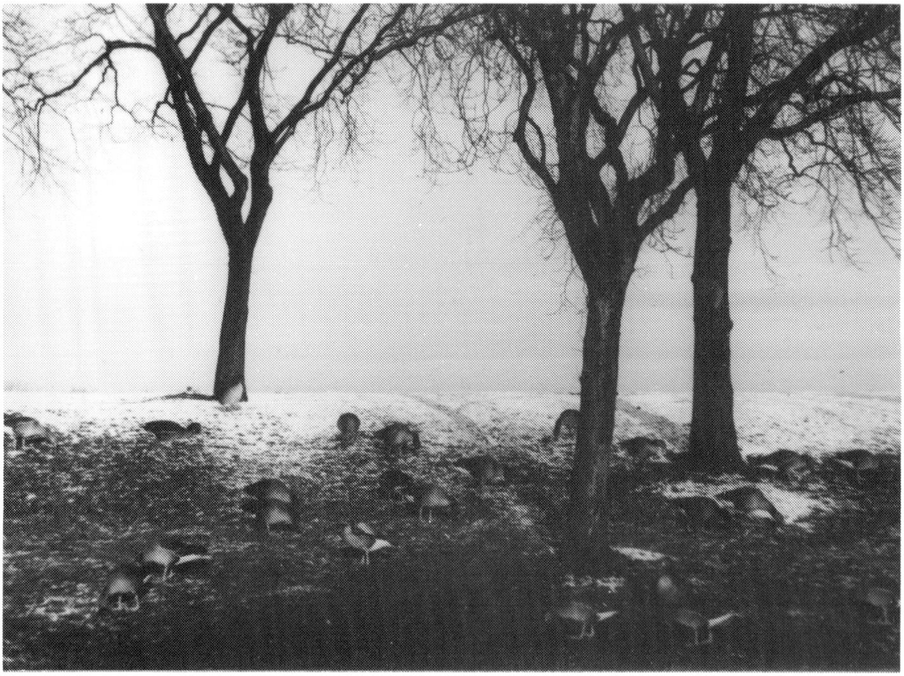

DECEMBER 12th

Geese now feed among the gulls,
glad of meadow grass
when once they spanned the northern wilderness.

The darkening sky is darkened by
their multitudinous flight,
as around the hill they uttering wheel.

A spaniel ran among them as
they fed, and they have risen
as one, alight, and feed again in flock.

Gulls, too, are circling
noisily by the window
as if there were agreement in dissent.

Celtic heads and beaks and knotted
necks with vivid eyes
have come to life around me.

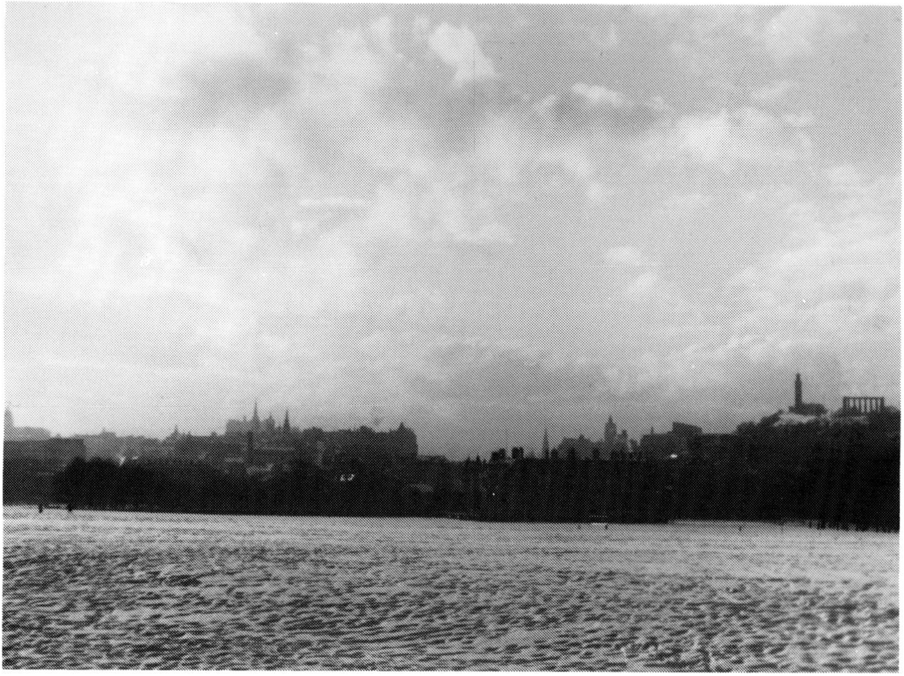

DECEMBER 24th

Apollo winters here:
strings his lyre like stars
through clouds, like swans
brightened in the wind:
practises his geometries
scaled to our particulars,
arcs, crags, promontories.

A coiled, constricted formula
translated into sections of our landscape,
our city-weathered hill;
reduced yet refined
from Delphic drama, grandeur
or golden Minoan harmony;
his circles here, triangles,
his proportions are coded
in our alpha rock,
our liquid sky, diagonal,
and huge, cold, omega, winter nights.

DECEMBER 31st

In my protection
    you lie sleeping
as I, wakeful,
    am in your keeping.
What the direction
    this boat may sail,
warily peaceful
    rain at the window
wind in crescendo
    moon-face full?

Raft for pilgrimage
    over the flood
made by arms crossed
    stronger than wood.
Casting anchorage
    each one alone
mourns what is lost,
    but charts the current
together this moment
    now, until dawn.

Geese are loud:
    nor stars nor our breathing
nor traffic's dirge
    compare with their weaving;
nor mountain nor cloud
    with their wingbeat cry
their swift surge
    and fine formation,
their navigation
    through sky on sky.

Soon I shall sleep
    without making plans;
the journey is longer
    for innocent ones.
If you would weep
    do not resist;
it will make you stronger
    like rain or goosefeather
or sorrow or death or
    branches or mist.

JANUARY 1st

We have crossed the threshold
into Time made new.
We make it new by stepping
bravely from the familiar
to proceed into a circle
narrower but higher
bearing with us
what we can,
all that ringed us what we are,
but opening this horizon
in each other
for our neighbour
by the truth of our endeavour.

JANUARY 5th

As daylight dims the stars
so consciousness is wakeful over dreams.

Turner's water-colours
are not exposed to view
except in Scotland's January,
month of darkness
when no strong light destroys them.

Winter discovers
what summer hides:
dreams, ancient magic,
fragile, water-colour feelings.

JANUARY 14th

> The moon:
> a pale clear twilight:
> seven geese wing eastward:
> dark omen of hope.

JANUARY 15th

> I hear the goddess of wind and rain
> hurtle around the mountain
> between trees
> against my high window.
>
> *'She passeth and goeth through all things*
> *by reason of her pureness'*
>
> Goddess of rivers and fountains
> geysers and hot springs:
> Sulis, unsullied
> *'she passeth through all things'*.
>
> The Romans called her *wisdom:*
> *'the highest goodness like water'*
> advises the Tao.
>
> Rain on my windows, Sulis,
> again this night, this dark,
> when we suffer the lag of winter
> before hope revives,
> loves confess.

JANUARY 23rd

Snow is falling
in that wind howling
the moon a coppery glow . . .

falls not on the city
but on the mountain
with circles of giant shadow . . .

despite his life-loving
my friend is dying
his wisdom silent and pale . . .

the skyline is fading
as snow is outlining
the contours and tracks of the hill . . .

my friend is dying
the wind is howling
the poem he lived is complete . . .

calm in the morning
daylight's revealing
poetry darkness has made.

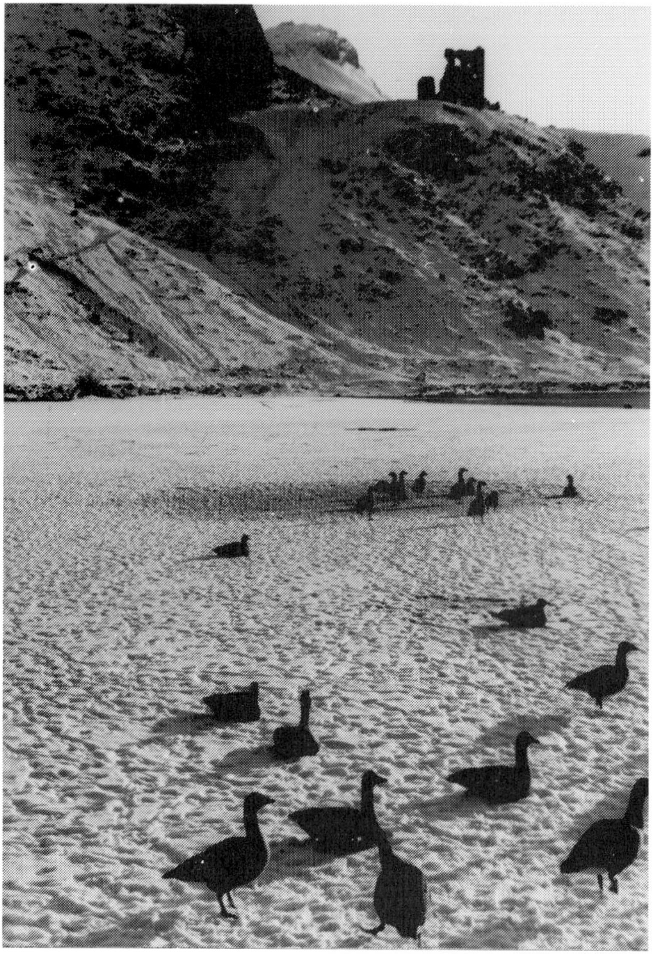

FEBRUARY 1st

Snow
the loch white
and black, where birds drink:
geese, swans, ducks, golden eye and moorhens,
coots, gulls, pigeons
walk on snowy ice.

The water has no edge.

Toboggans churn the milky snow
with slaps of laughter, shouts,
dogs, kids,
creaming the afternoon
in blinding sun, deafening speed.

A puppy is carried;
toddlers cling to mothers on the sledge
who bump and swerve and fall and go again
like girls, like children.

Cars wait while geese cross the road
cackling but unhurried;
they circumfly the hill, the houses and the road
and land again where water used to be;
they sit heavy-breasted in the snow
and dab thirsty beaks.

FEBRUARY 14th

The scene is set for me daily.
Again and again I paint it
as if an icon:
shall I make the cloak of the Virgin red?
How much to incline her head?
What proportion of sky
and cherubim, if any?
Where the square trap
door that leads to Hell?

Today's beauty lacks mercy:
calm, pale, unperturbed
in sleet, hail, keen wind.
Show it by nothing:
the hard edge of Hell's cliff,
by the very vacancy:
a walker straining forward
like dog on leash
but his dog unleashed in the wind.

Or shall I paint the mountain
as an elephant-god
fat, sleek, pregnant,
feet turned up
navel protruding
and wide, flat ears?
He is detached from predicaments
of weather or winter;
laughingly knows of desire's flame
never quenched to nirvana,
but lit anew in rock and sinew
year by year.

He is complete, content to be
gross, yet noble,
inevitable yet enabling.

FEBRUARY 24th

Tracks, ruts, footprints
birds, dogs, boots
decorate the silent, empty, shining, snowy park
where geese collect beneath the trees
and one dog gambols.

Beside the park
new-born babies sleep in see-through cribs;
delicate as snowflakes
born in a blizzard
children of white.

They herald the return of life:
as yet no mark, no print
on their soft perfection.

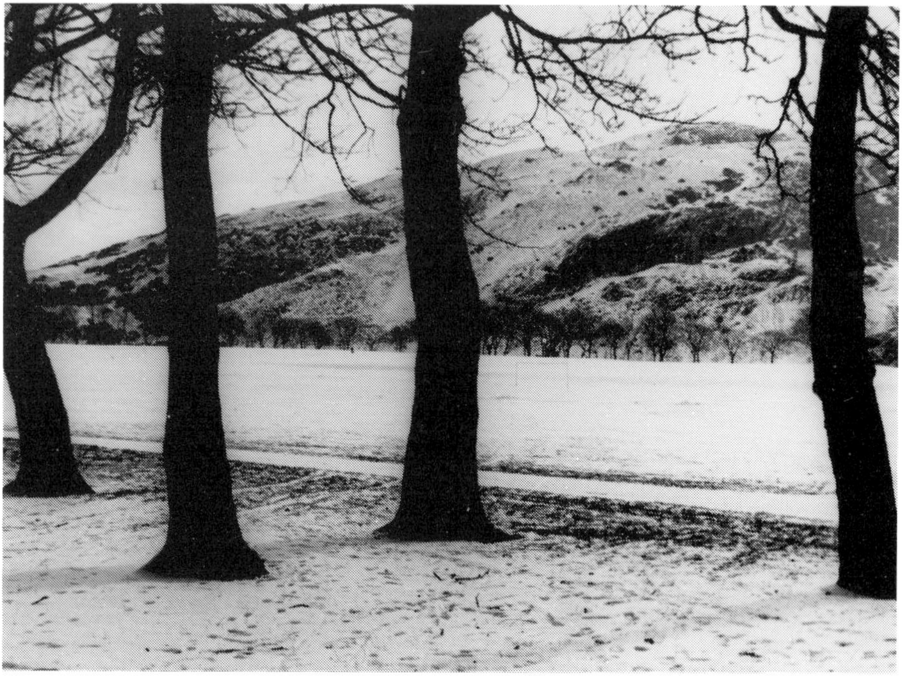

MARCH 9th

The geese have gone.

I saw them
walking under the trees
not feeding, walking,
and wondering if it was time.

They must have judged
that day was equal to night,
warm was level with cold,
the loch now too small
for fledged ambition.

The geese have gone.

No-one saw them leave.

They did not think, they flew
and somewhere in the guts of a gale
they are winging
heavy body steady
beak pointing ahead

as they cry into the wind
and keep formation
at last to sink again
by some wide stretch of melting lake,
their undebated, undesired
yet undoubted destination.

MOONLIGHT OVER ARTHUR'S SEAT

Tonight the mountain has laid aside solidity:
    earth that has jutted and cragged its way into sky
with trapped molten intensities pushed to their utmost reach
    then cooled and folded, crumpled into shadows.

Those massive columns now dissolve again in light
    wanly drawn about their huge shoulders,
concentrated in an act of illumination
    with here and there a shaded boundary.

Such exchange of substance noiselessly continues,
    comprehends each separate, weightless leaf,
each sweep of wilderness, each casual broken stone
    that shiningly betrays the eyes of gods.

From their intimate gaze we seek a sheen of protection
    yet, as they probe our levels of hidden light
we wager another moment towards our destiny
    and wrap ourselves in the sleep of our own courage.